NASH Diet

A Complete Guide to Boosting Your Liver, Glowing from Within and Revitalizing Your Health

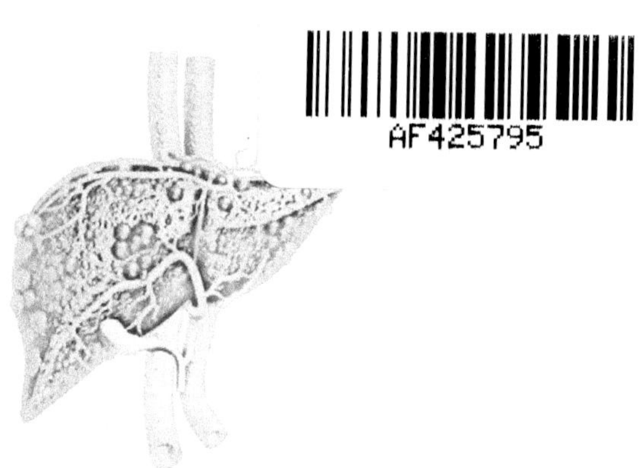

Michèle COHEN

LIABILITY DISCLAIMER

The information contained herein is not intended to replace professional medical advice. Any action taken on the basis of the contents is at the sole discretion and responsibility of the reader.

Readers should always consult appropriate healthcare professionals regarding any matter related to their health and well-being before taking any action concerning a health problem.

The information presented in this book represents the views of the publisher as of the date of publication. The publisher reserves the right to modify and update their opinions in light of new information. This book is published for informational purposes only. The author and publisher assume no liability for any liabilities arising from the use of this information. Although every effort has been made to verify the provided information, the author and publisher cannot accept responsibility for any errors, inaccuracies, or omissions.

CONTENTS

INTRODUCTION

Welcome to The Essential Guide to the NASH Diet, a book designed to help you understand and effectively manage non-alcoholic fatty liver disease (NASH). Whether you've recently been diagnosed with NASH, want to prevent its onset, or are simply looking to improve your liver health, this book is your ideal companion for navigating the complexities of this disease and adopting a healthy lifestyle.

NASH has become a major health problem worldwide, affecting millions of people of all ages and from all walks of life. It is characterized by the excessive accumulation of fat in the liver, associated with inflammation and liver damage. If left untreated, NASH can progress to cirrhosis, liver failure, and other serious complications.

This book is designed to provide you with an in-depth understanding of NASH and guide you step-by-step in adopting a diet adapted to this disease. You'll discover the fundamentals of the NASH diet, foods to prefer and avoid, beneficial dietary supplements, and practical advice for effective disease management.

In subsequent chapters, we'll explore the scientific basis of NASH, examining risk factors, underlying mechanisms, and potential complications. We will also discuss the links between NASH and other health problems such as type 2 diabetes, obesity, and cardiovascular disease.

Next, we'll look at the different aspects of the NASH diet. You'll discover which foods, rich in antioxidants, omega-3 fatty acids, lean proteins, whole grains, and legumes, can support your liver health. Plus, we'll give you tips on how to limit saturated fats, added sugars, processed foods, and alcohol, which can worsen NASH.

We'll also explore the role of dietary supplements in managing NASH, providing you with information on liver-friendly herbs, essential vitamins, and minerals needed for liver health. We'll give you advice on how to choose and use these supplements safely and effectively.

Furthermore, we'll provide you with delicious, NASH-friendly recipes and complete meal plans to help you put the principles of the diet into practice in your daily life. We're convinced that the NASH diet can be both beneficial to your health and enjoyable for your taste buds.

Finally, the book will also include inspiring testimonials from real people who have successfully improved their liver health by following the NASH diet. Their stories will provide you with motivation and encouragement on your own journey to better health.

Are you ready to take control of your liver health and adopt a nourishing lifestyle? This book is your complete guide to understanding, managing, and living successfully with non-alcoholic fatty liver disease. Together, let's explore the transformative potential the NASH diet can offer your health and well-being.

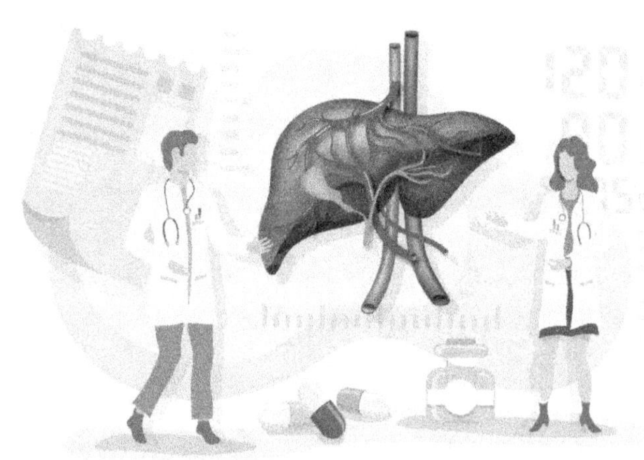

UNDERSTANDING NASH

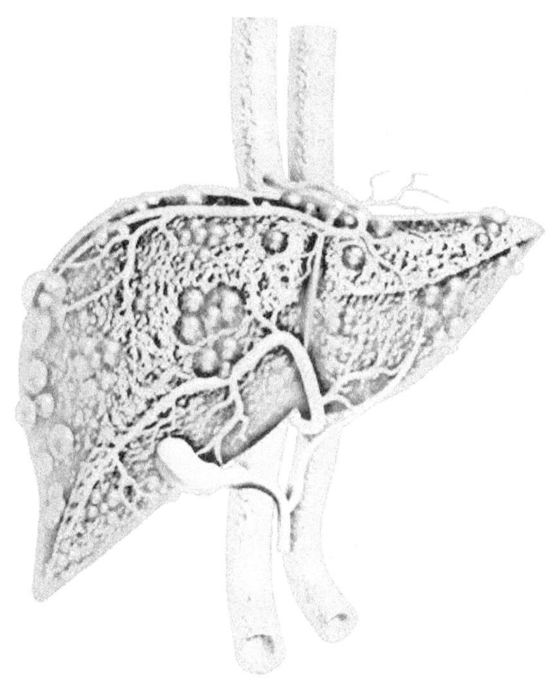

What is NASH?

The non-alcoholic metabolic syndrome of fatty liver (NASH) is an advanced form of non-alcoholic fatty liver (NAFLD). Unlike simple hepatic steatosis, which is characterized by an accumulation of fat in the liver, NASH involves inflammation and more severe liver damage. This inflammation can lead to liver fibrosis, cirrhosis and even liver cancer.

NASH has become a major public health concern, due to its growing incidence worldwide. It is estimated that 20–30% of the world's population suffers from NAFLD, and of these cases, around 20% will develop NASH.

Causes and Mechanisms of NASH

NASH is a multifactorial disease, resulting from the complex interplay of genetic, metabolic and environmental factors. The main causes and risk factors associated with NASH are:

- **Obesity:** Excess weight, particularly abdominal fat, is one of the main risk factors for NASH. Obesity is closely linked to insulin resistance and fat accumulation in the liver.
- **Insulin resistance:** Insulin resistance, a metabolic disorder common in obese people and those with type 2 diabetes, is strongly associated with the development of NASH.

- **Genetic factors:** Certain genetic variations may increase susceptibility to NASH. Studies have identified genes involved in lipid metabolism, inflammation and liver fibrosis.
- **Unbalanced diet:** A diet high in saturated fats, added sugars and processed foods is associated with an increased risk of developing NASH. Diets low in fiber and essential nutrients can also contribute to disease progression.

Symptoms and Complications of NASH

In its early stages, NASH is often asymptomatic, making early diagnosis difficult. However, as the disease progresses, certain symptoms may appear, such as:

- Persistent fatigue
- Pain or discomfort in the right upper abdomen
- loss of appetite
- Unintentional weight loss

Potential complications of NASH include liver fibrosis, cirrhosis (scarring of liver tissue), liver failure and liver cancer. These complications can lead to serious and even life-threatening health problems.

Accurate diagnosis of NASH requires a thorough evaluation including:

- **Blood tests:** Liver function tests, liver enzymes, inflammatory markers and fibrosis evaluation tests can be performed to assess liver damage.
- **Medical imaging:** Techniques such as ultrasonography, computed tomography (CT) or magnetic resonance imaging (MRI) can be used to assess fat accumulation in the liver, detect fibrosis and rule out other liver disorders.
- **Liver biopsy:** In some cases, a liver biopsy may be required to assess the severity of inflammation, fibrosis and the presence of lesions.

Once the diagnosis of NASH has been established, a comprehensive assessment of associated comorbidities and risk factors is essential, in order to develop a comprehensive management of the disease.

As NASH is a complex disease, management often involves a multidisciplinary approach. Current treatment options for NASH include:

- **Lifestyle modifications:** Lifestyle changes are considered the mainstay of NASH treatment. This includes weight loss, a balanced and healthy diet, regular exercise and stopping alcohol consumption.
- **Medications:** Some drug options can be used to treat specific aspects of NASH, such as insulin resistance, inflammation or liver fibrosis. However, there are currently no drugs specifically approved for the treatment of NASH.
- **Surgical interventions:** In cases of advanced cirrhosis or liver failure, liver transplantation may be considered.

Research into NASH is ongoing, and promising new treatments are in development. It is important to work closely with healthcare professionals to develop a personalized treatment plan based on disease severity and individual needs.

By understanding the essential aspects of NASH, you'll be able to make informed decisions to manage your liver health and adopt a suitable diet and lifestyle to control and improve your condition.

BASICS OF A HEALTHY DIET

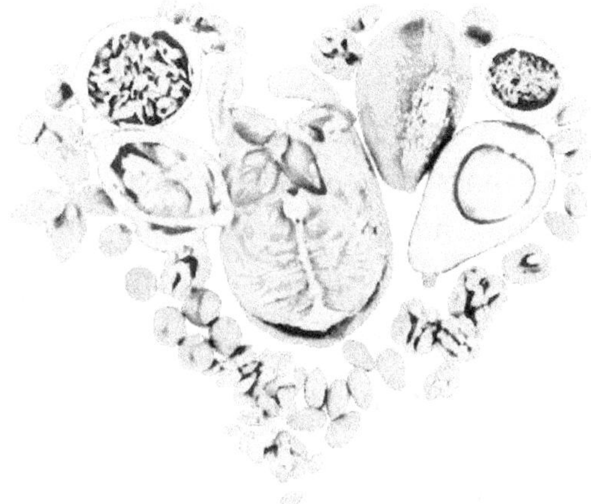

Now that you have a solid understanding of NASH, it's time to explore the fundamentals of a healthy diet to support your liver health. In this chapter, we'll cover the key elements of a balanced diet and how to adapt them specifically to NASH.

Essential Macronutrients

Macronutrients, which include carbohydrates, proteins and fats, are the main constituents of our diet. Understanding how to balance these macronutrients is crucial to maintaining good health, especially in the case of NASH.

- **Carbohydrates:** Carbohydrates are an important source of energy, but it's essential to choose the right types. Choose complex carbohydrates such as whole grains, vegetables, legumes and fruit, rather than refined carbohydrates such as baked goods and sweets.
- **Protein:** Protein is essential for tissue repair and growth. Choose lean protein sources such as fish, skinless poultry, low-fat dairy products, eggs and legumes. Limit consumption of fatty meats and cold cuts.
- **Lipids:** Lipids play an important role in maintaining cellular health and hormone regulation. Choose healthy fats, such as the monounsaturated fatty acids found in olive oil, avocados and walnuts, as well as the

polyunsaturated fatty acids found in oily fish, flaxseed and walnuts.

Essential Micronutrients

In addition to macronutrients, micronutrients such as vitamins and minerals are essential for maintaining optimal body function. Here are some key points to remember:

- **Vitamins:** Be sure to eat a variety of colorful fruits and vegetables to get a range of vitamins, including vitamins A, C, D, E and K. If necessary, consider supplements to fill nutritional gaps.
- **Minerals:** Minerals such as calcium, iron, magnesium and zinc are important for various metabolic processes. A balanced diet including dairy products, green vegetables, whole grains and legumes can help you meet your mineral requirements.

The importance of hydration and dietary fiber

In addition to the nutrients mentioned above, two essential elements to include in your NASH diet are adequate hydration and dietary fiber.

- **Hydration:** Be sure to drink enough water throughout the day to maintain proper hydration. Water helps eliminate toxins and support optimal liver function.
- **Dietary fiber:** Dietary fiber is beneficial for digestive health and blood sugar regulation. Choose fiber-rich foods such as fruits, vegetables, legumes and whole-grain cereals.

Foods to avoid or limit

As part of the NASH diet, it's important to limit or avoid certain foods that can aggravate the disease:

- **Foods high in saturated and trans fats:** Reduce your intake of fried foods, fatty meats, high-fat dairy products and processed foods containing trans fats.
- **Added sugars:** Limit foods and beverages containing added sugars, such as sweetened beverages, desserts and sweets.
- **Alcohol:** Avoid alcohol altogether, as it can aggravate the liver damage associated with NASH.

The importance of moderation and consistency

Finally, it's important to note that moderation and consistency are essential for a healthy, sustainable diet. Adopt a balanced and realistic approach to eating, focusing on nutritious foods most of the time, while allowing yourself occasional indulgences from time to time.

A balanced diet tailored to NASH is a key element in the management of this disease. By following the basic principles of a healthy diet, avoiding harmful foods and maintaining adequate hydration, you can support your liver health and improve your overall well-being.

FOODS TO CHOOSE ON THE NASH DIET

Diet plays a crucial role in the management of NASH. In this chapter, we'll explore specific foods that are beneficial for liver health and should be prioritized in the diet of people with NASH.

Antioxidant-Rich Vegetables and Fruit

Vegetables and fruit are essential components of a healthy diet for NASH due to their high fiber, vitamin, mineral and antioxidant content. The antioxidants found in these foods can help reduce inflammation and protect liver cells. Here are a few examples of foods to choose from:

- **Spinach:** Spinach is rich in vitamins A, C and K, as well as antioxidants such as lutein and zeaxanthin, which can protect the liver from oxidative damage.
- **Broccoli:** Broccoli contains sulfur compounds and flavonoids, which have antioxidant and anti-inflammatory properties beneficial to liver health.
- **Berries:** Berries, such as blueberries and raspberries, are rich in antioxidants, fiber and vitamins, making them nutritious choices for supporting liver health.

Sources of lean protein, such as fish and poultry

Protein is essential for overall health and liver recovery. However, it's important to favor lean protein sources in the NASH diet to reduce saturated fat and cholesterol intake. Here are some examples of foods to include:

- **Oily fish:** Oily fish, such as salmon, mackerel and sardines, are rich in omega-3 fatty acids, which have anti-inflammatory effects and can support liver health.
- **Poultry:** Poultry, such as skinless chicken and turkey, provide a source of lean protein without the addition of saturated fats. It's best to eat skinless cuts of meat and prepare them in a healthy way, such as baking or grilling.

Foods Rich in Liver-Friendly omega-3 Fatty Acids

Omega-3 fatty acids are beneficial fats for liver health. They have anti-inflammatory properties and can help reduce fat accumulation in the liver. Here are some omega-3-rich foods to include in your diet:

- **Vegetable oils:** Vegetable oils rich in omega-3, such as flaxseed oil, hempseed oil and walnut oil, can be used as seasoning in salads or for low-temperature cooking.
- **Chia and flax seeds:** Chia and flax seeds are rich in omega-3 fatty acids. Sprinkle them on cereals and salads, or add them to smoothies to boost your omega-3 intake.

Whole grains and legumes are sources of complex carbohydrates and fiber, making them beneficial for NASH management. They help maintain stable blood sugar levels and promote satiety. Here are some examples of foods to include:

- **Quinoa:** Quinoa is a seed rich in protein and fiber. It can be used as an alternative to refined grains and added to salads, side dishes or used as a base for meals.
- **Lentils and beans:** Lentils and beans are excellent sources of vegetable protein, fiber and essential nutrients. They can be used in soups, stews, salads or as main ingredients in vegetarian dishes.

The NASH diet should include antioxidant-rich vegetables and fruits, lean protein sources, foods rich in omega-3 fatty acids and whole grains and legumes. These foods provide essential nutrients to support liver health, reduce inflammation and promote optimal metabolic balance.

FOODS TO AVOID ON THE NASH DIET

When it comes to managing NASH, it's important to know which foods to avoid, as they can worsen inflammation, hepatic steatosis and liver damage. In this chapter, we'll look at specific foods that should be limited or avoided in the diet of people with NASH.

Foods Rich in Saturated and Trans Fats

Saturated and trans fats are known to raise LDL ("bad") cholesterol levels and promote fat accumulation in the liver. Here are a few examples of foods rich in saturated and trans fats to avoid:

- **Fatty meats:** Fatty meats, such as red meat, bacon, deli meats and processed meat products, are often rich in saturated fats. It's best to choose lean cuts of meat and limit consumption of these foods.
- **High-fat dairy products:** High-fat dairy products, such as butter, cream and full-fat cheeses, can contain high levels of saturated fat. Choose low-fat or fat-free versions instead.
- **Fried foods:** Fried foods, such as French fries, doughnuts and breaded foods, often contain trans fats from the oil used for frying. Reduce your consumption of fried foods as much as possible.

Processed foods and added sugars are often high in empty calories, refined sugars and saturated fats. They can contribute to excess weight, high blood sugar levels and fat accumulation in the liver. Here are some examples of foods to avoid:

- **Snacks and sugary drinks:** Soft drinks, sweetened fruit juices, energy drinks and sugary snacks, such as cookies, cakes and candy, are high in added sugars and empty calories. Choose healthier alternatives instead, such as water, fruit infusions or fresh fruit snacks.
- **Sugar-rich processed foods:** Processed foods such as sweet cereals, commercial sauces, chocolate bars and pre-packaged desserts often contain added sugars. Read nutrition labels carefully and choose low-sugar or no-sugar-added options.

Alcohol consumption can have adverse effects on liver health, particularly in people with NASH. Alcohol can aggravate inflammation, hepatic steatosis and liver damage. It is recommended to avoid alcohol consumption altogether if you have NASH.

As part of the NASH diet, it's important to avoid foods high in saturated and trans fats, processed foods and added sugars, as well as alcohol. By limiting these foods and making healthy food choices, you can support liver health, reduce inflammation and promote optimal metabolic balance.

DIETARY SUPPLEMENTS FOR NASH

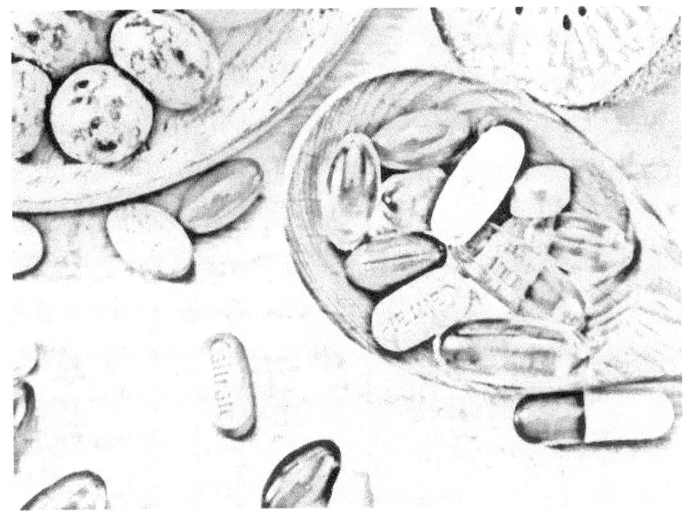

As part of the management of NASH, certain dietary supplements can be beneficial for liver health. In this chapter, we'll look at herbal supplements, essential vitamins and minerals, and the precautions to be taken when taking dietary supplements.

Herbal Supplements Beneficial to the Liver

Some herbs have beneficial properties for liver health and can be used in the form of dietary supplements. Here are just a few examples of herbal supplements that can help in the management of NASH:

- **Milk thistle (Silybum marianum):** Milk thistle has long been used to support liver health. It contains an active compound called silymarin, which has antioxidant and anti-inflammatory properties. Milk thistle can help reduce inflammation and protect the liver from damage.
- **Turmeric (Curcuma longa):** Turmeric is a spice widely used in Indian cuisine. It contains an active compound called curcumin, which has anti-inflammatory and antioxidant properties. Turmeric can help reduce inflammation and protect the liver.
- **Dandelion (Taraxacum officinale):** Dandelion is a plant commonly used to support liver health. It has diuretic

properties and can help stimulate bile production, promoting liver detoxification.

It's important to note that the use of herbal supplements should be discussed with a healthcare professional, as they may interact with other medications or have adverse effects.

Vitamins and minerals essential for liver health

Certain vitamins and minerals play an important role in liver health and can be taken as dietary supplements. Here are just a few examples of essential vitamins and minerals:

- **Vitamin E:** Vitamin E is a powerful antioxidant that can help reduce inflammation and protect liver cells from damage. It can be taken as a dietary supplement, but it's important to stick to recommended doses, as excessive amounts can be harmful.
- **Vitamin D:** Vitamin D is important for general health, and may also have beneficial effects on liver health. It can be obtained from moderate sun exposure and certain foods, but in some cases, a dietary supplement may be necessary to maintain adequate levels.
- **Zinc:** Zinc is an essential mineral that plays a role in many bodily functions, including

liver health. It can help reduce inflammation and support liver function. Zinc supplementation may be considered if deficiencies are identified.

It's important to take certain precautions when taking dietary supplements, including those designed for liver health. Here are a few points to consider:

- **Consult a healthcare professional:** Before starting any dietary supplement, it's advisable to consult a healthcare professional, such as a physician or nutritionist, who can advise you on your specific needs.
- **Respect recommended doses:** It is essential to follow the dosage instructions supplied with dietary supplements and not to exceed recommended doses, as excessive amounts can be hazardous to your health.
- **Be aware of drug interactions:** Some dietary supplements can interact with drugs, so it's important to report any medications you're taking to your healthcare professional.
- **Choose quality products:** Make sure you choose quality dietary supplements from

reputable sources that have been tested for efficacy and safety.

Some dietary supplements, such as those with liver-benefiting herbs, vitamins and essential minerals, can be helpful in managing NASH. However, it is important to take these supplements under the supervision of a healthcare professional, and to observe the precautions necessary to ensure their safety and efficacy.

WEIGHT MANAGEMENT STRATEGIES FOR NASH

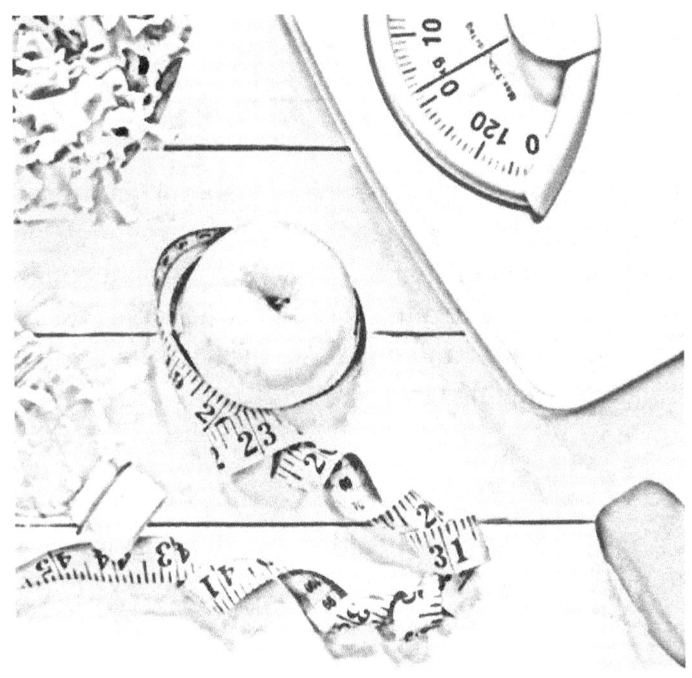

Weight management plays a crucial role in the management of NASH, as obesity and overweight are major risk factors for this disease. In this chapter, we will explore effective strategies for weight loss and maintenance of a healthy weight in the context of NASH.

Setting Realistic Weight Loss Goals

When it comes to weight loss, it's important to set realistic, achievable goals. It's best to aim for gradual weight loss, averaging 0.5 to 1 kg per week. Losing weight too quickly can have adverse effects on your health and increase the risk of weight regain in the long term.

Adopt a Balanced, Calorie-Controlled Diet

To lose weight in a healthy way, it's essential to follow a balanced, calorie-controlled diet. Here are some key principles to follow:

- **Reduce calorie intake:** Calculate your daily calorie intake required for weight loss and reduce it slightly. This can be achieved by controlling portions, choosing lower-calorie foods and limiting foods rich in fats and sugars.
- **Focus on nutritious foods:** Focus on nutrient-rich foods such as fruits, vegetables, whole grains, lean proteins and healthy fat sources. These foods are low in

calories and provide your body with essential nutrients.

- **Practice moderation:** Adopt a balanced approach by including a variety of foods in your diet, while controlling portions. Learn to recognize your body's hunger and satiety signals.

Exercise and Regular Physical Activity

In addition to a balanced diet, regular physical activity is essential for weight loss and maintaining a healthy weight. Here are a few recommendations:

- **Consult a healthcare professional:** Before starting an exercise program, it's important to consult a healthcare professional to assess your physical condition and obtain personalized recommendations.
- **Choose activities you enjoy:** Choose physical activities you enjoy to maintain your motivation over the long term. This could include walking, swimming, cycling, dancing or any other exercise you enjoy.
- **Aim for regular activity:** Try to exercise regularly, ideally at least 150 minutes a week of moderate-intensity activity. Spread your activity throughout the week to reap the maximum benefits.

Chronic stress and lack of sleep can negatively affect weight management. Here are some tips for managing these factors:

- **Adopt stress management techniques:** Practice activities such as meditation, yoga, deep breathing or any other method that helps you reduce stress.
- **Prioritize quality sleep:** Make sure you get enough sleep every night, as lack of sleep can influence hunger and satiety hormones. Establish a regular sleep routine and create an environment conducive to rest.

Follow-up and Professional Support

To optimize your weight loss and NASH management results, it can be beneficial to work closely with healthcare professionals, such as a nutritionist, doctor or life coach. They can provide personalized advice, support and regular follow-up to help you achieve your goals.

Weight management is an essential aspect of NASH management. By adopting a balanced diet, engaging in regular physical activity, managing stress and getting adequate sleep, you can progress towards a healthy weight and improve your overall health.

STRATEGIES FOR MANAGING STRESS AND PROMOTING WELL-BEING

Chronic stress can have a negative impact on liver health and worsen NASH symptoms. In this chapter, we'll explore effective strategies for managing stress, promoting emotional well-being and supporting liver health.

Understanding the Link Between Stress and NASH

Chronic stress can trigger inflammatory responses in the body, which can worsen the liver damage associated with NASH. Understanding this relationship is key to implementing effective stress management strategies.

Stress Management Techniques

Meditation and mindfulness: Meditation and the practice of mindfulness can help reduce stress by focusing attention on the present moment and cultivating a state of inner calm. There are many apps and online resources to guide you in these practices.

- **Physical activity:** Regular exercise is an excellent way to reduce stress. Choose an activity you enjoy, such as walking, running, yoga or dance, and make it part of your daily routine.
- **Relaxation techniques:** Explore different relaxation techniques, such as deep breathing, visualization, yoga or stretching.

Find the one that suits you best and practice it regularly to reduce your stress levels.

Emotional and Social Support

Talk to a mental health professional: If you're feeling overwhelmed by stress, don't hesitate to consult a mental health professional, such as a psychologist or therapist. They can help you develop stress management strategies tailored to your situation.

Social support: Don't underestimate the power of social support. Talk about your concerns with trusted loved ones, join support groups or participate in social activities that allow you to connect with others.

Promoting General Well-being

Adequate sleep: Sleep plays a crucial role in managing stress and promoting well-being. Make sure you have a regular sleep routine, create an environment conducive to rest and practice healthy sleep habits.

- **Balanced diet:** A healthy, balanced diet can support your emotional well-being. Choose nutritious foods, avoid processed foods and added sugars, and focus on nutrient-rich foods that support liver health.
- **Leisure and pleasurable activities:** Make time for activities you enjoy, whether it's

reading, music, painting, gardening or any other creative or recreational activity that gives you pleasure and allows you to relax.

Stress management and the promotion of well-being are essential elements in the management of NASH. By adopting stress management techniques, seeking emotional and social support, and promoting a balanced lifestyle, you can reduce the impact of stress on your liver health and improve your overall well-being.

MEDICAL FOLLOW-UP AND MULTIDISCIPLINARY CARE

Managing NASH requires regular medical follow-up and a multidisciplinary approach to optimize results and support liver health. In this chapter, we'll discuss the importance of medical follow-up, screening tests and the team of healthcare professionals who can support you on your journey.

Regular Medical Check-ups

Regular medical follow-up is crucial to monitoring the progression of NASH and adjusting the treatment plan accordingly. Your doctor plays a key role in this process and can perform the following actions:

- **General health assessment:** Your doctor will perform regular physical examinations, assess your symptoms and monitor your overall health.
- **Liver function tests:** Liver function tests, such as blood tests, may be performed to assess your liver function and monitor markers of inflammation and liver damage.
- **Abdominal ultrasound or other imaging tests:** Imaging tests may be performed to assess fat accumulation in the liver, detect hepatic fibrosis and evaluate the condition of your liver.

In addition to regular medical examinations, certain screening tests may be recommended to assess the extent of liver damage and the risk of complications. These tests may include:

- **Liver biopsy:** A liver biopsy may be performed to assess the degree of fibrosis and inflammation in the liver. However, this procedure can be invasive, and other non-invasive methods are often preferred.
- **FibroScan or liver stiffness tests:** These non-invasive tests measure liver stiffness and can provide information on the presence of hepatic fibrosis.
- **Advanced laboratory tests:** Some more advanced laboratory tests, such as fibrosis markers or inflammation tests, can be used to assess liver condition more accurately.

Team of healthcare professionals

A multidisciplinary approach involving a team of healthcare professionals can help you manage NASH effectively. Here are some of the team members who may be involved:

- **Gastroenterologist or hepatologist:** These specialists are trained to diagnose and treat liver disease, including NASH. They will be responsible for your medical follow-up and the overall management of your condition.

- **Nutritionist or dietician:** A nutritionist or dietician can help you develop an eating plan adapted to NASH and your specific needs, while providing appropriate nutritional advice.
- **Physical activity educator:** A physical activity educator can help you develop an exercise program tailored to your abilities and goals, while ensuring that you engage in physical activity safely and effectively.
- **Psychologist or mental health counselor:** Emotional support is important in managing NASH, and a psychologist or mental health counselor can help you cope with the emotional challenges associated with your condition.
- **Primary care team:** Your family physician and other members of your primary care team can also play an important role in coordinating your care, managing medications and monitoring your overall health.

Regular medical follow-up, appropriate screening tests and a multidisciplinary team of healthcare professionals are essential for the effective management of NASH. Working closely with these professionals will enable you to optimize your treatment, monitor your condition and make informed decisions to support your liver health.

STRATEGIES FOR MANAGING STRESS AND MAINTAINING A HEALTHY LIFESTYLE IN THE NASH DIET

Stress and lifestyle play a crucial role in the management of NASH. In this chapter, we'll discuss strategies for managing stress, maintaining a healthy lifestyle and supporting liver health as part of the NASH diet.

Managing Stress

Stress can have a negative impact on liver health and worsen NASH symptoms. It's important to implement effective strategies to manage stress. Here are some useful approaches:

- **Relaxation techniques:** Meditation, deep breathing, yoga and other relaxation techniques can help reduce stress and promote a state of calm and well-being.
- **Regular physical activity:** Exercise is an excellent way to reduce stress. Take up a regular physical activity that you enjoy, such as walking, swimming, cycling or dancing.
- **Time management:** Plan your schedule effectively to avoid feeling overwhelmed. Prioritize your tasks and learn to say no when necessary.

Balanced Diet

A balanced diet is essential for maintaining good liver health in NASH. Here are some tips for a healthy diet:

- **Consume fiber-rich foods:** Dietary fiber aids digestion, reduces inflammation and helps maintain a healthy weight. Include vegetables, fruit, whole grains and legumes in your diet.
- **Limit added sugars:** Added sugars can aggravate inflammation and fatty liver. Reduce your intake of sweetened beverages, sugary snacks and processed foods rich in added sugars.
- **Focus on healthy fats:** Healthy fats, such as the omega-3 fatty acids found in oily fish, nuts and seeds, are beneficial for liver health. Limit saturated fats and avoid trans fats.

Maintaining a Healthy Weight

Maintaining a healthy weight is essential in the management of NASH, as excess weight can worsen hepatic steatosis and inflammation. Here are some tips for maintaining a healthy weight:

- **Eat a balanced diet and control portions:** Eat balanced meals that include lean proteins, vegetables, fruits and whole grains. Control portions to avoid excess calories.
- **Exercise regularly:** Physical activity is essential to maintaining a healthy weight. Find an activity you enjoy and do it

regularly, ideally for at least 30 minutes a day.

- **Balance diet and physical activity:** Make sure you consume enough calories to support your energy needs, taking into account your level of physical activity.

As part of the NASH diet, it's important to manage stress, adopt a balanced diet and maintain a healthy weight. These strategies help support liver health, reduce inflammation and promote a healthy, balanced lifestyle.

THE IMPORTANCE OF REGULAR MEDICAL MONITORING IN THE NASH DIET

Regular medical follow-up plays an essential role in the management of NASH. In this chapter, we will discuss the importance of regular medical follow-up, frequently recommended examinations and tests, and the role of the healthcare professional in the management of NASH.

The Importance of Regular Medical Follow-up

Regular medical follow-up is essential to monitor your health, evaluate the effectiveness of treatment and make any necessary adjustments. Here are a few reasons why regular medical follow-up is important in NASH:

- **Assessment of overall health:** Your healthcare professional will perform a complete physical examination to assess your overall health, including evaluation of your liver, weight, blood pressure, cholesterol levels, etc.
- **Monitoring the progression of NASH:** Regular tests and examinations allow us to monitor the progression of your NASH, detect any complications and take appropriate action.
- **Adjusting your treatment plan:** Your healthcare professional will be able to adjust your treatment plan according to your specific needs, taking into account your changing health and test results.

Various examinations and tests may be recommended as part of regular medical follow-up for NASH. Here are some of the examinations and tests frequently recommended:

- **Blood tests:** Blood tests are used to assess levels of certain liver enzymes, inflammatory markers, blood lipids, vitamins, minerals and so on. These tests help assess liver function and detect any abnormalities.
- **Abdominal ultrasound:** Abdominal ultrasound visualizes the liver and assesses the presence of hepatic steatosis or other structural abnormalities.
- **Fibroscan:** Fibroscan is a non-invasive test that assesses liver fibrosis by measuring liver stiffness.
- **Liver biopsy:** In some cases, a liver biopsy may be recommended to assess the extent of fibrosis and inflammation. However, other non-invasive methods are increasingly being used to replace biopsy.

The Role of the Healthcare Professional

Your healthcare professional, whether a physician, hepatologist, nutritionist or other specialist, plays a key role in the management of NASH. They are there to guide and support you every step of the way. Here are some of the important roles they play:

- **Establishing an accurate diagnosis:** Your healthcare professional will conduct a complete health assessment, take your medical history and perform the necessary examinations and tests to establish an accurate diagnosis of your NASH.
- **Develop a personalized treatment plan:** Based on your health status and test results, your healthcare professional will develop a personalized treatment plan, including dietary recommendations, physical activity advice and, if necessary, medication.
- **Provide regular follow-up:** Your healthcare professional will provide regular follow-up to assess treatment effectiveness, monitor your health and make any necessary adjustments.
- **Provide advice and support:** Your healthcare professional is there to answer your questions, provide advice on lifestyle, diet and dietary supplements, and support you throughout your NASH management journey.

Regular medical follow-up is essential in the management of NASH. It allows you to monitor your health, evaluate the effectiveness of treatment and make any necessary adjustments. Work closely with your healthcare professional to ensure optimal follow-up and support on your NASH management journey.

Patient Self-Management and Involvement

In addition to regular medical follow-up, it's important for patients to play an active role in managing their NASH. Self-management involves making healthy lifestyle choices and being aware of the impact of eating habits and physical activity on liver health. Here are some important aspects of self-management in NASH:

- **Adopt a healthy diet:** Following a balanced diet rich in vegetables, fruits, whole grains, lean proteins and healthy fats is essential in managing NASH. Avoiding processed foods high in saturated fats and added sugars is also recommended.
- **Maintain a healthy weight:** Obesity and overweight are major risk factors for NASH. It is therefore crucial to maintain a healthy weight by adopting healthy eating habits and regular physical activity.
- **Exercise regularly:** Physical activity plays an important role in the management of NASH. It can help reduce inflammation, improve insulin sensitivity and promote weight loss. At least 150 minutes of moderate-intensity activity per week is recommended.

- **Avoid alcohol and toxic substances:** Alcohol is particularly harmful to the liver, so it's crucial to avoid or significantly limit its consumption. It is also important to avoid exposure to other toxic substances that can damage the liver.
- **Managing stress:** Chronic stress can have a negative impact on liver health. It's important to develop stress management techniques, such as meditation, deep breathing, yoga or other relaxing activities.
- **Follow medical recommendations:** It's essential to follow your healthcare professionals recommendations regarding medications, dietary supplements and other aspects of your treatment plan.

Self-management plays a crucial role in managing NASH. By adopting healthy lifestyle choices, monitoring diet, engaging in regular physical activity and avoiding harmful substances, patients can actively contribute to the preservation of their liver health. Working closely with your healthcare professional and maintaining regular follow-up is essential for optimal management of NASH.

Support and Resources for People With NASH

Living with NASH can be challenging, but it's important to know that there are resources and support available to help you on your journey. In this section, we'll discuss some of the resources that can be helpful for people with NASH:

- **Support groups:** Support groups can provide a safe space to share your experiences, ask questions and get emotional support from people going through similar situations. Joining a local or online support group can enable you to connect with other people with NASH and benefit from their advice and support.
- **Associations and organizations:** There are associations and organizations dedicated to NASH awareness and research. These organizations often provide resources, up-to-date information and advice for people with NASH. Familiarizing yourself with these organizations can help you find valuable information and stay up to date on advances in the field.
- **Nutritional consulting services:** Working with a nutrition professional who specializes in liver disease can help you develop an eating plan tailored to your specific condition. These professionals can provide personalized advice on nutrition, dietary supplements and weight management strategies.
- **Mental health services:** Living with a chronic disease like NASH can have an impact on your emotional well-being. It may be helpful to consult a mental health

professional, such as a psychologist or counselor, for emotional support and stress management strategies.

- **Online resources:** the Internet is full of online resources, such as websites, blogs and forums, which can provide useful information and perspectives shared by other people with NASH. However, it's important to check the reliability of information sources and consult your healthcare professional for advice specific to your case.

It's important to seek out and use the resources and support available to people with NASH. Support groups, associations, nutritional counseling services, mental health services and online resources can all play a vital role in your NASH management journey. Don't hesitate to explore these resources and surround yourself with a strong support network to accompany you along the way.

FUTURE PROSPECTS FOR NASH TREATMENT

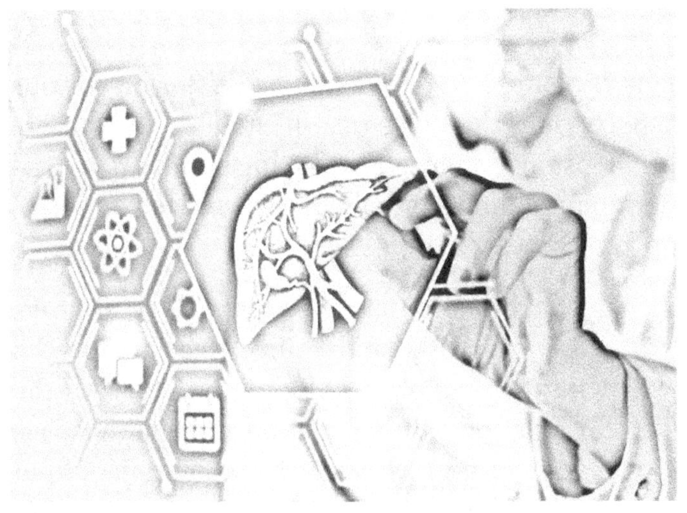

The treatment of NASH is a constantly evolving field of research, with many promising prospects for the future. In this chapter, we explore some of the advances and future prospects in the treatment of NASH.

Current Research

Research into NASH is ongoing, focusing on various aspects of the disease, including its origin, progression, underlying mechanisms and potential therapeutic interventions. Here are a few areas of ongoing research:

- **Pharmacological therapies:** Several drugs are currently under investigation for the treatment of NASH. Some target the reduction of inflammation and liver fibrosis, while others focus on the regulation of lipid and insulin metabolism. These drugs are being evaluated in clinical trials to assess their efficacy and safety.
- **Targeted therapies:** Research is also exploring targeted therapies that specifically target the molecular processes involved in the development of NASH. These therapeutic approaches may include inhibitors of certain enzymes or drugs that act on specific metabolic pathways.
- **Gene therapies:** Gene therapy is an emerging field in the treatment of NASH. It aims to modify the expression of genes

implicated in the disease to alleviate inflammation, fibrosis and fat accumulation in the liver.

Non-Pharmacological Approaches

In addition to pharmacological therapies, certain non-pharmacological approaches are also being studied for the treatment of NASH. These approaches include:

- **Nutritional therapy:** Specific diets, such as the Mediterranean diet, rich in fruits, vegetables, whole grains and healthy fats, are being studied for their impact on NASH. Studies are also evaluating the effect of certain bioactive compounds, such as polyphenols, on inflammation and hepatic steatosis.
- **Exercise therapy:** Regular physical activity is known for its benefits on general health, including liver health. Studies are exploring the effect of different types of exercise on the progression of NASH and the underlying mechanisms.
- **Complementary therapies:** Some complementary therapies, such as acupuncture, herbal medicine and specific dietary supplements, are also being investigated for their potential in the management of NASH. However, further

research is needed to assess their efficacy and safety.

The Importance of Prevention

Finally, it's worth emphasizing the importance of prevention in the fight against NASH. Adopting a healthy lifestyle, including a balanced diet, regular physical activity, weight management and avoidance of alcohol and toxic substances, can help prevent the development and progression of NASH.

Research into NASH is progressing rapidly, opening up new perspectives in the treatment of this disease. Pharmacological approaches, non-pharmacological approaches and prevention are all important areas of study. As research advances, it is hoped that new effective and targeted therapies will emerge to help people with NASH manage their disease more effectively.

LIVING WITH NASH— QUALITY OF LIFE AND WELL-BEING

NASH is a chronic disease that can have a significant impact on the quality of life and well-being of those affected. In this chapter, we will look in detail at the various aspects related to quality of life and well-being for patients living with NASH.

Managing Symptoms and Complications

Managing the symptoms and complications associated with NASH is essential to improving patients' quality of life. Some common symptoms of NASH include fatigue, loss of appetite, abdominal pain and confusion. Your healthcare professional may prescribe specific medications or treatments to relieve these symptoms and improve your comfort.

It's also important to monitor and manage the potential complications of NASH, such as liver cirrhosis, portal hypertension or diabetes, working closely with your medical team.

Emotional and psychological support

Living with a chronic disease like NASH can be an emotionally challenging experience. Patients may face feelings of anxiety, depression, frustration and stress related to their condition. Emotional and psychological support is essential to cope with these challenges. You may consider consulting a mental health professional, such as a psychologist or counselor, who can help you develop stress management strategies, overcome anxiety and improve your overall psychological well-being.

Support groups can also be a valuable resource, offering a safe space to share your experiences with others living with NASH and receive mutual support.

Lifestyle adaptation

Lifestyle adaptation is often necessary to manage NASH and improve quality of life. This includes adjustments in diet, physical activity and daily habits. Adopting a healthy, balanced diet can help maintain a healthy weight, reduce inflammation and support liver health. Working with a nutrition professional can help you develop an eating plan tailored to your specific health condition.

Regular physical activity is also important, as it can help improve energy, liver function and emotional well-being.

Talk to your healthcare professional for recommendations on the types of exercise and intensity levels that are right for you.

Education and independence

Education about NASH and an understanding of your own condition are essential to empowering yourself and taking charge of your life. Take the time to learn about key aspects of NASH, such as its causes, progression, treatments and self-management strategies.

Your healthcare professional can be an excellent source of information, but you can also consult reliable online resources, specialized books or join patient associations for up-to-date information.

By better understanding your disease, you'll be able to make informed decisions and actively participate in your own care.

Prevention and regular follow-up

Prevention plays a crucial role in the management of NASH. In addition to lifestyle adjustments, it's important to avoid known risk factors such as excessive alcohol consumption, smoking and the use of potentially liver-toxic medications.

In addition, regular follow-up with your healthcare professional is essential to monitor disease progression, adjust treatments if necessary and manage potential complications. Regular follow-up helps to detect early signs of NASH progression and to intervene quickly.

Living with NASH can be challenging, but there are strategies and resources that can improve patients' quality of life and well-being. Symptom management, emotional support, lifestyle adaptation, education and prevention are key to living fully with NASH. Don't forget to consult your healthcare professional for appropriate advice and follow-up throughout your journey.

HOLISTIC APPROACHES TO NASH MANAGEMENT

Managing NASH involves more than just the medical and physical aspects. A holistic approach that considers the whole individual—body, mind and soul—can play an important role in managing the disease. In this chapter, we explore some holistic perspectives that can complement traditional medical treatments.

Relaxation and Stress Management Techniques

Stress can have a negative impact on the health and progression of NASH. Learning and practicing relaxation techniques such as deep breathing, meditation, yoga or sophrology can help reduce stress, promote emotional well-being and improve quality of life. These techniques can help calm the mind, reduce anxiety and promote relaxation, which can benefit overall body and liver health.

Complementary and Alternative Approaches

Some complementary and alternative approaches, such as acupuncture, chiropractic, homeopathy or naturopathy, can be explored in the management of NASH. These approaches focus on restoring the body's balance and vital energy, and can be used to complement traditional medical treatments. It is important to consult a qualified healthcare professional before undertaking these approaches to ensure their safety and compatibility with your condition.

Social Support and Community Connection

Social support and community connection play a crucial role in managing NASH. Participating in support groups, getting involved in community activities or turning to friends and loved ones can provide emotional support, practical advice and a sense of belonging. NASH-specific support groups can offer a space to share your experiences, ask questions and get advice from people who understand what you're going through. Connecting with others living with NASH can provide mutual support and help you navigate the challenges associated with the disease.

Self-care and General Well-being

Taking care of yourself in a holistic way can help improve NASH management. This includes a balanced diet, regular physical activity, adequate sleep, enriching leisure activities, as well as time and priority management. Adopting good lifestyle habits can strengthen your immune system, increase your energy, improve your mood and support your overall health. It's important to listen to your body's needs, allow yourself moments of rest and relaxation, and engage in activities that bring you joy and well-being.

Integrating Spirituality

For some people, integrating spirituality can play a significant role in managing NASH. Whether through religious practice, meditation, prayer, personal development or connection with nature, spirituality can bring emotional support, a perspective of meaning and inner strength to the NASH journey. Finding spiritual practices that nourish and ground you can help you face the challenges of the disease and maintain a positive, resilient attitude.

The holistic approach to managing NASH takes into account the whole individual. Relaxation techniques, complementary approaches, social support, self-care and the integration of spirituality can complement traditional medical treatments and contribute to a better quality of life and overall well-being. It's important to explore these perspectives while respecting your own beliefs and finding what works best for you in your NASH management journey. Don't hesitate to seek help from qualified healthcare professionals and surround yourself with a support network to accompany you throughout this process.

FUTURE PROSPECTS IN NASH RESEARCH

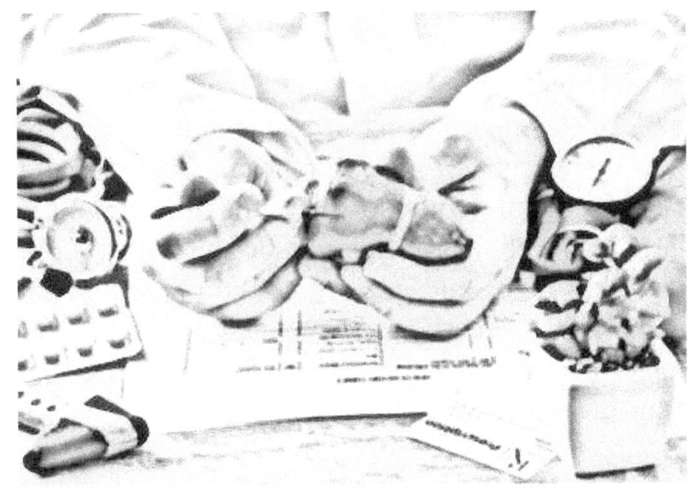

NASH is a complex and constantly evolving disease, and research in this field is advancing rapidly. In this chapter, we'll look at future prospects in NASH research, including scientific advances, emerging therapies and challenges ahead.

Scientific Advances

Researchers are striving to better understand the underlying mechanisms of NASH and to identify new therapeutic targets. Significant advances have been made in understanding the inflammation, fatty liver and liver fibrosis associated with NASH. Genetic studies and gene expression analyses are helping to identify genetic risk factors and molecular signatures specific to NASH, paving the way for personalized treatments.

Emerging Therapies

Several emerging therapies are currently being studied for the treatment of NASH. These include GLP-1 (glucagon-like peptide 1) receptor agonists, HSD17B13 serine protease inhibitors, FXR (farnesoid X receptor) agonists and bile acid catabolism inhibitors. These drugs target the metabolic, inflammatory and fibrotic processes involved in NASH, with the aim of slowing or reversing disease progression. Ongoing clinical trials are providing promising data on their efficacy and safety.

Research Challenges

Despite the progress made, NASH research faces a number of challenges. The complexity of the disease and the diversity of individual responses to treatment make drug discovery and development difficult. In addition, diagnostic criteria and outcome evaluation criteria in clinical trials need to be standardized to facilitate comparison of results between studies. Researchers are also faced with the need to better understand the mechanisms of disease progression, specific risk factors and the complex interactions between the liver and other organs.

Multidisciplinary Approaches

Research into NASH requires a multidisciplinary approach, with collaboration between scientists, clinicians, genetics, immunology, hepatology and nutrition researchers. The establishment of research consortia shared databases and international collaborations helps to accelerate research and maximize available resources.

Hope for a Cure

Although many advances have been made, there is as yet no cure for NASH. However, advances in research and emerging therapies hold out the hope of a cure in the future. It is essential that research continues and that ongoing investment is made to tackle this disease effectively.

Research into NASH is progressing rapidly, opening up new perspectives in the understanding, diagnosis and treatment of the disease. Scientific advances, emerging therapies, research challenges and multidisciplinary approaches are all helping to improve the management of NASH. It's important to keep abreast of the latest advances and maintain open communication with your healthcare professional to benefit from the most up to date and appropriate treatment options for you.

NASH RECIPES FOR HEALTHY AND DELICIOUS EATING

In this chapter, we offer a selection of recipes specially designed for people with NASH. These recipes focus on foods beneficial to liver health, with an emphasis on vegetables, fruits, lean proteins, whole grains and omega-3 fatty acids. They are designed to be tasty, balanced and easy to prepare.

Berry and Chia Seed Breakfast Bowl

Ingredients:

- 1 cup mixed berries (strawberries, blueberries, raspberries)
- 2 tablespoons chia seeds
- ½ cup Greek yogurt (choose low-fat or non-fat options)
- 2 tablespoons chopped nuts (almonds, walnuts, or pecans)

Instructions:

In a bowl, mash half of the mixed berries with a fork to release their juices.

Stir in the chia seeds and let the mixture sit for about 10 minutes to allow the chia seeds to absorb the liquid.

Add the Greek yogurt on top of the chia seed mixture.

Sprinkle the remaining mixed berries and chopped nuts over the yogurt.

Enjoy this refreshing and nutrient-packed breakfast bowl.

Spinach and Mushroom Egg White Omelet

Ingredients:

- 4 egg whites
- 1 cup fresh spinach leaves
- ½ cup sliced mushrooms
- ¼ teaspoon dried herbs (such as basil, thyme, oregano)
- Salt and pepper to taste
- 1 teaspoon olive oil

Instructions:

In a non-stick skillet, heat the olive oil over medium heat. Add the mushrooms and sauté until they are softened.

Add the spinach leaves and cook until wilted.

In a separate bowl, whisk the egg whites with the dried herbs, salt, and pepper.

Pour the egg white mixture over the cooked vegetables in the skillet.

Cook the omelet until the edges are set and the center is slightly runny.

Carefully fold the omelet in half and cook for another minute until fully set.

Serve this protein-packed omelet with a side of whole-grain toast or fresh salad.

Spinach and Mushroom Omelette

Ingredients:

- 2 large eggs
- 1 cup fresh spinach leaves
- ½ cup sliced mushrooms
- ¼ cup diced onions
- ¼ cup diced bell peppers
- 1 teaspoon olive oil
- Salt and pepper to taste

Instructions:

In a bowl, beat the eggs until well combined. Set aside.

Heat the olive oil in a non-stick skillet over medium heat.

Add the onions and bell peppers to the skillet and sauté until they become slightly tender, about 3–4 minutes.

Add the mushrooms and spinach to the skillet and cook until the spinach wilts and the mushrooms are cooked through.

Season the vegetable mixture with salt and pepper.

Pour the beaten eggs over the vegetables in the skillet, ensuring they are evenly distributed.

Cook the omelette for about 3–4 minutes, or until the eggs are set.

Carefully fold the omelette in half and cook for an additional minute.

Slide the omelette onto a plate and serve hot.

This spinach and mushroom omelette is packed with nutrients and makes for a delicious and satisfying breakfast.

Banana Oat Pancakes

Ingredients:

- 1 ripe banana
- ½ cup rolled oats
- 2 tablespoons almond flour
- ½ teaspoon baking powder
- ¼ teaspoon ground cinnamon
- ¼ cup unsweetened almond milk (or any non-dairy milk of your choice)
- 1 teaspoon vanilla extract
- Coconut oil for cooking
- Fresh berries and a drizzle of honey for serving (optional)

Instructions:

In a blender or food processor, blend the ripe banana until smooth.

Add the rolled oats, almond flour, baking powder, ground cinnamon, almond milk, and vanilla extract to the blender. Blend until all the ingredients are well combined and form a smooth batter.

Heat a non-stick skillet or griddle over medium heat and lightly grease it with coconut oil.

Pour ¼ cup of the pancake batter onto the skillet, spreading it slightly into a circular shape.

Cook the pancake for about 2–3 minutes, or until bubbles start to form on the surface.

Flip the pancake and cook for an additional 1–2 minutes, until golden brown and cooked through.

Repeat with the remaining batter to make more pancakes.

Serve the banana oat pancakes warm, optionally topped with fresh berries and a drizzle of honey for added sweetness.

Quinoa Breakfast Porridge

Ingredients:

- ½ cup quinoa, rinsed
- 1 cup unsweetened almond milk (or any non-dairy milk of your choice)
- ½ teaspoon cinnamon
- ¼ teaspoon vanilla extract
- 1 cup fresh mixed berries
- 1 tablespoon honey or maple syrup (optional)

Instructions:

In a small saucepan, combine the quinoa, almond milk, cinnamon, and vanilla extract.

Bring the mixture to a boil over medium heat, then reduce the heat to low and simmer for 15–20 minutes until the quinoa is cooked and the liquid is absorbed.

Stir occasionally to prevent sticking.

Remove from heat and let it cool for a few minutes.

Serve the quinoa porridge in bowls, topped with fresh mixed berries and a drizzle of honey or maple syrup, if desired.

Enjoy this warm and nutritious breakfast porridge to start your day off right.

Greek Yogurt Parfait

Ingredients:

- 1 cup plain Greek yogurt
- ¼ cup granola (choose a low-sugar option)
- ¼ cup mixed fresh berries
- 1 tablespoon honey or maple syrup (optional)
- Chopped nuts for garnish (optional)

Instructions:

In a glass or bowl, layer the Greek yogurt, granola, and mixed fresh berries.

Repeat the layers until all the ingredients are used.

Drizzle honey or maple syrup over the top if desired, for added sweetness.

Garnish with chopped nuts for an extra crunch, if desired.

This Greek yogurt parfait is a nutritious and filling breakfast option that can be customized with your favorite fruits and toppings.

Grilled Salmon with Lemon-Dill Sauce

Ingredients:

- 4 salmon fillets (about 4–6 ounces each)
- Juice of 1 lemon
- 2 tablespoons chopped fresh dill
- Salt and pepper to taste

For the Lemon-Dill Sauce:

- ½ cup Greek yogurt
- Juice of ½ lemon
- 1 tablespoon chopped fresh dill
- 1 clove garlic, minced
- Salt and pepper to taste

Instructions:

Preheat the grill to medium-high heat.

Season the salmon fillets with lemon juice, chopped dill, salt, and pepper.

Grill the salmon for about 4–5 minutes on each side until cooked through and flaky.

While the salmon is grilling, prepare the lemon-dill sauce by combining all the sauce ingredients in a small bowl and mixing well.

Serve the grilled salmon with a dollop of the lemon-dill sauce on top.

Pair with a side of roasted vegetables, such as asparagus or broccoli, for a complete and healthy meal.

Mediterranean Quinoa Salad

Ingredients:

- 1 cup cooked quinoa
- 1 cup cherry tomatoes, halved
- 1 cup diced cucumber
- ½ cup pitted olives (Kalamata or black olives), halved
- ¼ cup crumbled feta cheese
- 2 tablespoons chopped fresh parsley
- Juice of 1 lemon
- 2 tablespoons extra-virgin olive oil
- Salt and pepper to taste

Instructions:

In a large mixing bowl, combine the cooked quinoa, cherry tomatoes, cucumber, olives, feta cheese, and parsley.

In a separate small bowl, whisk together the lemon juice, olive oil, salt, and pepper.

Pour the dressing over the quinoa mixture and toss well to combine.

Adjust the seasoning according to your taste preferences.

Allow the salad to sit for at least 15 minutes to allow the flavors to meld.

Serve this refreshing Mediterranean quinoa salad as a light lunch or side dish alongside grilled chicken or fish.

91

Baked Chicken Breast with Roasted Sweet Potatoes

Ingredients:

- 2 boneless, skinless chicken breasts
- 1 teaspoon olive oil
- 1 teaspoon paprika
- ½ teaspoon garlic powder
- ½ teaspoon dried thyme
- Salt and pepper to taste

For the Roasted Sweet Potatoes:

- 2 medium sweet potatoes, peeled and cut into cubes
- 1 tablespoon olive oil
- ½ teaspoon ground cumin
- ¼ teaspoon chili powder
- Salt and pepper to taste

Instructions:

Preheat the oven to 400 °F (200 °C).

Place the chicken breasts on a baking sheet lined with parchment paper.

Drizzle the chicken breasts with olive oil and sprinkle with paprika, garlic powder, dried thyme, salt, and pepper.

In a separate bowl, toss the sweet potato cubes with olive oil, ground cumin, chili powder, salt, and pepper.

Arrange the sweet potato cubes on the same baking sheet as the chicken breasts.

Bake for 20–25 minutes or until the chicken is cooked through and the sweet potatoes are tender.

Remove from the oven and let the chicken rest for a few minutes before slicing.

Serve the baked chicken breast with a generous portion of roasted sweet potatoes for a satisfying and nutritious meal.

Lentil and Vegetable Curry

Ingredients:

- 1 cup dried green or brown lentils
- 1 tablespoon olive oil
- 1 onion, chopped
- 2 cloves garlic, minced
- 1-inch piece of ginger, grated
- 1 tablespoon curry powder
- 1 teaspoon ground cumin
- 1 teaspoon ground turmeric
- 1 teaspoon paprika
- 1 can diced tomatoes (14 ounces)
- 2 cups vegetable broth
- 2 cups mixed vegetables (such as bell peppers, zucchini, carrots, and peas)
- Salt and pepper to taste
- Fresh cilantro for garnish (optional)
- Cooked brown rice or quinoa for serving

Instructions:

Rinse the lentils under cold water and set aside.

Heat the olive oil in a large pot over medium heat.

Add the chopped onion, garlic, and grated ginger, and sauté until the onion is translucent.

Stir in the curry powder, cumin, turmeric, and paprika, and cook for another minute to toast the spices.

Add the diced tomatoes (with their juices) and vegetable broth to the pot, stirring well.

Add the lentils and mixed vegetables to the pot and bring to a boil.

Reduce the heat to low, cover, and simmer for 20–25 minutes, or until the lentils and vegetables are tender.

Season with salt and pepper to taste.

Serve the lentil and vegetable curry over cooked brown rice or quinoa.

Garnish with fresh cilantro, if desired, for an extra burst of flavor.

Lentil and Vegetable Soup

Ingredients:

- 1 cup dried red lentils
- 1 tablespoon olive oil
- 1 onion, chopped
- 2 cloves garlic, minced
- 2 carrots, chopped
- 2 celery stalks, chopped
- 1 zucchini, chopped
- 1 can diced tomatoes (14 ounces)
- 4 cups vegetable broth
- 1 teaspoon ground cumin
- 1 teaspoon dried thyme
- Salt and pepper to taste
- Fresh parsley for garnish (optional)

Instructions:

Rinse the red lentils under cold water and set aside.

Heat the olive oil in a large pot over medium heat.

Add the chopped onion, minced garlic, carrots, celery, and zucchini to the pot. Sauté until the vegetables are slightly softened.

Add the diced tomatoes (with their juices), vegetable broth, red lentils, ground cumin, dried thyme, salt, and pepper to the pot. Stir well to combine.

Bring the soup to a boil, then reduce the heat to low and simmer for about 20–25 minutes, or until the lentils and vegetables are tender.

Adjust the seasoning if needed.

Serve the lentil and vegetable soup hot, garnished with fresh parsley, if desired. Enjoy this comforting and nutritious soup as a light lunch or dinner option.

Quinoa-Stuffed Bell Peppers

Ingredients:

- 4 bell peppers (any color), tops removed and seeds removed
- 1 cup cooked quinoa
- 1 cup diced tomatoes
- 1 cup cooked black beans
- ½ cup corn kernels
- ¼ cup chopped fresh cilantro
- 1 teaspoon ground cumin
- ½ teaspoon chili powder
- Salt and pepper to taste
- ¼ cup shredded cheddar cheese (optional)

Instructions:

Preheat the oven to 375 °F (190 °C).

In a mixing bowl, combine the cooked quinoa, diced tomatoes, black beans, corn kernels, chopped cilantro, ground cumin, chili powder, salt, and pepper. Mix well.

Stuff each bell pepper with the quinoa mixture, pressing it down gently.

Place the stuffed bell peppers in a baking dish and cover with foil.

Bake for 25–30 minutes, or until the bell peppers are tender and the filling is heated through.

If desired, remove the foil and sprinkle shredded cheddar cheese on top of each bell pepper. Return to the oven for an additional 5 minutes, or until the cheese is melted and bubbly.

Remove from the oven and let the stuffed bell peppers cool slightly before serving.

These quinoa-stuffed bell peppers are a flavorful and wholesome option for a satisfying meal.

Salmon and Vegetable Stir-Fry

Ingredients:

- 2 salmon fillets
- 2 tablespoons low-sodium soy sauce
- 1 tablespoon honey
- 1 tablespoon rice vinegar
- 1 tablespoon cornstarch
- 1 tablespoon olive oil
- 2 cloves garlic, minced
- 1 teaspoon grated ginger
- 1 red bell pepper, sliced
- 1 yellow bell pepper, sliced
- 1 cup snap peas
- 1 cup broccoli florets
- Salt and pepper to taste
- Sesame seeds for garnish (optional)

Instructions:

In a small bowl, whisk together the soy sauce, honey, rice vinegar, and cornstarch to make the sauce. Set aside.

Heat the olive oil in a large skillet or wok over medium-high heat.

Season the salmon fillets with salt and pepper, then add them to the skillet. Cook for about 4–5 minutes per side, or until cooked to your desired level of doneness. Remove the salmon from the skillet and set aside.

In the same skillet, add the minced garlic and grated ginger. Sauté for about 1 minute, until fragrant.

Add the sliced bell peppers, snap peas, and broccoli florets to the skillet. Stir-fry for about 3–4 minutes, until the vegetables are crisp-tender.

Pour the sauce over the vegetables and stir well to coat. Cook for an additional 2 minutes, until the sauce has thickened.

Slice the cooked salmon into pieces and add it back to the skillet. Gently toss to combine with the vegetables and sauce.

Serve the salmon and vegetable stir-fry hot, garnished with sesame seeds if desired. Enjoy this flavorful and nutrient-rich dish!

Quinoa and Black Bean Salad

Ingredients:

- 1 cup cooked quinoa
- 1 can black beans (15 ounces), rinsed and drained
- 1 cup diced tomatoes
- 1 cup diced cucumbers
- ½ cup diced red onion
- ¼ cup chopped fresh cilantro
- Juice of 1 lime
- 2 tablespoons extra-virgin olive oil
- Salt and pepper to taste

Instructions:

In a large mixing bowl, combine the cooked quinoa, black beans, diced tomatoes, diced cucumbers, diced red onion, and chopped cilantro.

In a separate small bowl, whisk together the lime juice, olive oil, salt, and pepper.

Pour the dressing over the quinoa mixture and toss well to combine. Adjust the seasoning according to your taste preferences.

Allow the salad to sit for at least 15 minutes to allow the flavors to meld.

Serve this refreshing quinoa and black bean salad as a light lunch or side dish.

Grilled Chicken and Vegetable Skewers

Ingredients:

- 2 boneless, skinless chicken breasts, cut into cubes
- 1 red bell pepper, cut into chunks
- 1 yellow bell pepper, cut into chunks
- 1 red onion, cut into chunks
- 8 cherry tomatoes
- 2 tablespoons olive oil
- 1 teaspoon dried oregano
- Salt and pepper to taste

Instructions:

Preheat the grill or grill pan to medium-high heat.

In a bowl, combine the chicken cubes, bell pepper chunks, onion chunks, cherry tomatoes, olive oil, dried oregano, salt, and pepper. Toss to coat everything evenly.

Thread the chicken and vegetables onto skewers, alternating between the ingredients.

Grill the skewers for about 10–12 minutes, turning occasionally, until the chicken is cooked through and the vegetables are tender.

Serve the grilled chicken and vegetable skewers with a side of quinoa or a mixed green salad for a complete and balanced meal.

Grilled Vegetable Skewers with Balsamic Glaze

Ingredients:

- 1 zucchini, cut into rounds
- 1 yellow squash, cut into rounds
- 1 red onion, cut into chunks
- 1 bell pepper (any color), cut into chunks
- 8 cherry tomatoes
- 2 tablespoons balsamic vinegar
- 1 tablespoon olive oil
- 1 tablespoon honey
- Salt and pepper to taste

Instructions:

Preheat the grill or grill pan to medium-high heat.

In a small bowl, whisk together the balsamic vinegar, olive oil, honey, salt, and pepper to make the glaze.

Thread the zucchini rounds, yellow squash rounds, red onion chunks, bell pepper chunks, and cherry tomatoes onto skewers, alternating the vegetables.

Brush the vegetable skewers with the balsamic glaze, coating them evenly.

Grill the skewers for about 10–12 minutes, turning occasionally and brushing with more glaze, until the vegetables are tender and lightly charred.

Remove from the grill and let them cool slightly before serving.

These grilled vegetable skewers with balsamic glaze make a delightful and colorful addition to any meal.

Roasted Vegetable Quinoa Bowl

Ingredients:

- 1 cup cooked quinoa
- 1 small sweet potato, peeled and diced
- 1 small zucchini, diced
- 1 small red bell pepper, diced
- 1 cup broccoli florets
- 2 tablespoons olive oil
- 1 teaspoon smoked paprika
- ½ teaspoon garlic powder
- Salt and pepper to taste
- Fresh parsley for garnish (optional)

Instructions:

Preheat the oven to 400 °F (200 °C).

In a large mixing bowl, toss together the diced sweet potato, diced zucchini, diced red bell pepper, and broccoli florets with olive oil, smoked paprika, garlic powder, salt, and pepper.

Spread the vegetables out on a baking sheet in a single layer.

Roast for about 25–30 minutes, or until the vegetables are tender and lightly browned, stirring halfway through.

In a serving bowl, combine the roasted vegetables with the cooked quinoa.

Toss everything together until well mixed.

Garnish with fresh parsley, if desired.

This roasted vegetable quinoa bowl is a satisfying and nutritious meal that can be enjoyed warm or cold.

Greek Salad with Grilled Chicken

Ingredients:

- 2 boneless, skinless chicken breasts
- 4 cups mixed salad greens
- 1 cup cherry tomatoes, halved
- 1 cucumber, sliced
- ¼ red onion, thinly sliced
- ¼ cup Kalamata olives
- ¼ cup crumbled feta cheese
- 2 tablespoons extra-virgin olive oil
- 1 tablespoon red wine vinegar
- 1 teaspoon dried oregano
- Salt and pepper to taste

Instructions:

Preheat the grill or grill pan to medium-high heat.

Season the chicken breasts with salt, pepper, and dried oregano.

Grill the chicken for about 6–8 minutes per side, or until cooked through.

Let the chicken rest for a few minutes, then slice it into strips.

In a large salad bowl, combine the mixed salad greens, cherry tomatoes, cucumber slices, red onion slices, Kalamata olives, and crumbled feta cheese.

In a small bowl, whisk together the extra-virgin olive oil, red wine vinegar, dried oregano, salt, and pepper to make the dressing.

Drizzle the dressing over the salad and toss well to coat.

Top the salad with the grilled chicken strips.

This Greek salad with grilled chicken is a refreshing and protein-packed meal option.

Baked Cod with Lemon and Herbs

Ingredients:

- 2 cod fillets
- 2 tablespoons lemon juice
- 1 tablespoon olive oil
- 1 teaspoon dried dill
- 1 teaspoon dried thyme
- Salt and pepper to taste
- Lemon wedges for serving

Instructions:

Preheat the oven to 400 °F (200 °C).

Place the cod fillets in a baking dish and drizzle them with lemon juice and olive oil.

Sprinkle the dried dill, dried thyme, salt, and pepper evenly over the fillets.

Bake for about 12–15 minutes, or until the cod is opaque and flakes easily with a fork.

Serve the baked cod with lemon wedges on the side. This light and flavorful dish pairs well with steamed vegetables or a side salad.

Homemade Hummus with Veggie Sticks

Ingredients:

- 1 can chickpeas (15 ounces), rinsed and drained
- 2 tablespoons tahini
- Juice of 1 lemon
- 1 clove garlic, minced
- 2 tablespoons extra-virgin olive oil
- Salt and pepper to taste
- Assorted vegetable sticks (carrots, cucumber, bell peppers) for dipping

Instructions:

In a food processor, combine the chickpeas, tahini, lemon juice, minced garlic, and olive oil.

Process until smooth and creamy, adding a little water if needed to achieve the desired consistency.

Season with salt and pepper to taste.

Transfer the hummus to a serving bowl and drizzle with a little extra olive oil.

Serve with a platter of vegetable sticks for dipping.

Enjoy this healthy and protein-rich snack that's perfect for satisfying your midday cravings.

Baked Zucchini Fries

Ingredients:

- 2 medium zucchini, cut into sticks
- ½ cup whole wheat breadcrumbs
- ¼ cup grated Parmesan cheese
- ½ teaspoon dried Italian seasoning
- ¼ teaspoon garlic powder
- Salt and pepper to taste
- 1 large egg, beaten

Instructions:

Preheat the oven to 425 °F (220 °C).

In a shallow bowl, combine the breadcrumbs, grated Parmesan cheese, Italian seasoning, garlic powder, salt, and pepper. Dip each zucchini stick into the beaten egg, allowing any excess to drip off.

Roll the zucchini stick in the breadcrumb mixture, pressing gently to adhere.

Place the coated zucchini sticks on a baking sheet lined with parchment paper.

Bake for 20–25 minutes, or until the zucchini fries are golden and crisp. Remove from the oven and let them cool slightly before serving.

These baked zucchini fries are a healthier alternative to traditional fries and make a fantastic appetizer or snack option.

Roasted Chickpeas with Smoky Paprika

Ingredients:

- 1 can chickpeas (15 ounces), rinsed and drained
- 1 tablespoon olive oil
- 1 teaspoon smoked paprika
- ½ teaspoon ground cumin
- ¼ teaspoon garlic powder
- Salt and pepper to taste

Instructions:

Preheat the oven to 400 °F (200 °C).

Pat the rinsed and drained chickpeas dry with a clean kitchen towel or paper towels.

In a bowl, toss the chickpeas with olive oil, smoked paprika, ground cumin, garlic powder, salt, and pepper.

Spread the seasoned chickpeas in a single layer on a baking sheet lined with parchment paper.

Roast in the oven for 25–30 minutes, or until the chickpeas are golden brown and crispy.

Remove from the oven and let them cool completely before serving.

These roasted chickpeas make a crunchy and protein-packed snack that you can enjoy anytime.

Roasted Chickpeas

Ingredients:

- 1 can chickpeas, drained and rinsed
- 1 tablespoon olive oil
- 1 teaspoon paprika
- ½ teaspoon garlic powder
- ½ teaspoon cumin
- ¼ teaspoon salt
- ¼ teaspoon black pepper

Instructions:

Preheat the oven to 400 °F (200 °C) and line a baking sheet with parchment paper.

Pat the chickpeas dry using a paper towel to remove excess moisture.

In a bowl, toss the chickpeas with olive oil, paprika, garlic powder, cumin, salt, and black pepper until well coated.

Spread the seasoned chickpeas in a single layer on the prepared baking sheet.

Roast in the oven for about 25–30 minutes, stirring halfway through, until the chickpeas are golden brown and crispy. Remove from the oven and let them cool completely before serving.

These roasted chickpeas make a crunchy and protein-packed snack.

Zucchini Fritters

Ingredients:

- 2 medium zucchinis, grated
- ¼ cup finely diced onion
- ¼ cup almond flour
- 2 tablespoons grated Parmesan cheese
- 1 clove garlic, minced
- 1 large egg, beaten
- ½ teaspoon dried oregano
- ½ teaspoon salt
- ¼ teaspoon black pepper
- Olive oil for frying

Instructions:

Place the grated zucchinis in a clean kitchen towel and squeeze out as much excess moisture as possible.

In a mixing bowl, combine the grated zucchinis, diced onion, almond flour, Parmesan cheese, minced garlic, beaten egg, dried oregano, salt, and black pepper. Stir until well combined.

Heat a thin layer of olive oil in a skillet over medium heat.

Drop spoonfuls of the zucchini mixture into the hot skillet and flatten them slightly with a spatula.

Cook the fritters for about 3–4 minutes per side, or until golden brown and crispy.

Transfer the cooked fritters to a paper towel-lined plate to drain any excess oil.

Repeat the process with the remaining zucchini mixture.

Serve the zucchini fritters warm as a tasty appetizer or snack.

Cucumber and Hummus Bites

Ingredients:

- 1 English cucumber
- ½ cup hummus (choose a low-fat and low-sodium option)
- Fresh dill or parsley for garnish (optional)

Instructions:

Slice the cucumber into rounds, about ¼-inch thick.

Arrange the cucumber slices on a serving platter or plate.

Spoon a small dollop of hummus onto each cucumber slice.

Garnish with fresh dill or parsley if desired.

These cucumber and hummus bites are refreshing and make a light and healthy snack or appetizer option.

Mixed Berry Parfait

Ingredients:

- 1 cup Greek yogurt (choose low-fat or non-fat options)
- 1 cup mixed berries (strawberries, blueberries, raspberries)
- ¼ cup granola

Instructions:

In a glass or dessert dish, layer Greek yogurt, mixed berries, and granola.

Repeat the layers until all the ingredients are used, ending with a sprinkle of granola on top.

Serve immediately, or refrigerate for a few hours to allow the flavors to meld together.

This mixed berry parfait is a light and refreshing dessert option that satisfies your sweet tooth while providing a dose of antioxidants.

Dark Chocolate Avocado Mousse

Ingredients:

- 2 ripe avocados
- ¼ cup unsweetened cocoa powder
- ¼ cup honey or maple syrup
- ¼ cup unsweetened almond milk (or any non-dairy milk of your choice)
- 1 teaspoon vanilla extract
- Pinch of salt
- Dark chocolate shavings for garnish (optional)

Instructions:

In a blender or food processor, combine the avocados, cocoa powder, honey or maple syrup, almond milk, vanilla extract, and salt.

Blend until smooth and creamy, scraping down the sides as needed. Taste and adjust the sweetness if desired.

Transfer the chocolate avocado mousse to serving bowls or glasses. Refrigerate for at least 30 minutes to allow it to set.

Garnish with dark chocolate shavings, if desired, before serving.

This rich and indulgent dark chocolate avocado mousse is a healthier alternative to traditional chocolate desserts.

Baked Apples with Cinnamon and Walnuts

Ingredients:

- 2 apples (such as Granny Smith or Honeycrisp)
- 2 tablespoons chopped walnuts
- 1 tablespoon honey
- ½ teaspoon ground cinnamon
- ¼ teaspoon vanilla extract

Instructions:

Preheat the oven to 375 °F (190 °C).

Core the apples, removing the seeds and creating a hollow cavity in the center.

In a small bowl, mix together the chopped walnuts, honey, ground cinnamon, and vanilla extract.

Spoon the walnut mixture into the center of each apple, packing it down lightly.

Place the stuffed apples in a baking dish and bake for 25–30 minutes, or until the apples are tender.

Remove from the oven and let them cool for a few minutes before serving.

These baked apples with cinnamon and walnuts are a comforting and wholesome dessert option that's perfect for cooler evenings.

Berry Chia Pudding

Ingredients:

- ¼ cup chia seeds
- 1 cup unsweetened almond milk (or any non-dairy milk of your choice)
- 1 tablespoon honey or maple syrup
- ½ teaspoon vanilla extract
- 1 cup mixed berries (such as strawberries, blueberries, and raspberries)

Instructions:

In a bowl, combine the chia seeds, almond milk, honey or maple syrup, and vanilla extract. Stir well to combine.

Let the mixture sit for about 10 minutes, then stir again to prevent clumping.

Cover the bowl and refrigerate for at least 2 hours or overnight, allowing the chia seeds to absorb the liquid and form a pudding-like consistency.

When ready to serve, layer the chia pudding and mixed berries in serving glasses or bowls.

Garnish with additional berries if desired.

Enjoy this healthy and fiber-rich berry chia pudding as a delicious dessert or even as a nourishing breakfast option.

Baked Apples with Cinnamon and Almonds

Ingredients:

- 2 medium-sized apples (such as Granny Smith or Honeycrisp)
- 1 tablespoon unsalted butter or coconut oil, melted
- 2 tablespoons chopped almonds `
- 1 teaspoon ground cinnamon
- 1 teaspoon honey or maple syrup (optional)
- Plain yogurt or whipped cream for serving (optional)

Instructions:

Preheat the oven to 375 °F (190 °C).

Core the apples using an apple corer or a small knife, leaving the bottoms intact.

Place the cored apples in a baking dish.

In a small bowl, mix together the melted butter or coconut oil, chopped almonds, ground cinnamon, and honey or maple syrup (if using).

Spoon the almond mixture into the center of each apple, filling the cavities.

Bake the apples for about 25–30 minutes, or until they are tender and the filling is golden brown.

Remove from the oven and let them cool for a few minutes.

Serve the baked apples warm, optionally topped with a dollop of plain yogurt or whipped cream for added creaminess.

Chocolate Avocado Mousse

Ingredients:

- 2 ripe avocados
- ¼ cup unsweetened cocoa powder
- ¼ cup honey or maple syrup
- ¼ cup unsweetened almond milk (or any non-dairy milk of your choice)
- 1 teaspoon vanilla extract
- Pinch of salt
- Fresh berries for garnish (optional)

Instructions:

Cut the avocados in half, remove the pits, and scoop the flesh into a blender or food processor.

Add the cocoa powder, honey or maple syrup, almond milk, vanilla extract, and salt to the blender. Blend until smooth and creamy, scraping down the sides as needed.

Taste and adjust the sweetness if desired by adding more honey or maple syrup. Transfer the mousse to serving bowls or glasses.

Refrigerate for at least 30 minutes to allow the mousse to chill and set. Garnish with fresh berries if desired before serving.

Indulge in this rich and decadent chocolate avocado mousse guilt-free!

These NASH recipes offer a wide range of options for every meal of the day, ensuring that you can enjoy delicious and nutritious food while supporting your liver health. From nourishing breakfast bowls to satisfying main dishes and delectable desserts, there's something to suit every palate. Remember to make ingredient substitutions or modifications based on your dietary preferences or restrictions. With these recipes, you can embark on a culinary journey that nourishes your body and brings joy to your taste buds, all while promoting the reversal of Non-alcoholic Steatohepatitis. Happy cooking and happy eating!

SAMPLE MEAL PLANS FOR A SUCCESSFUL DAY

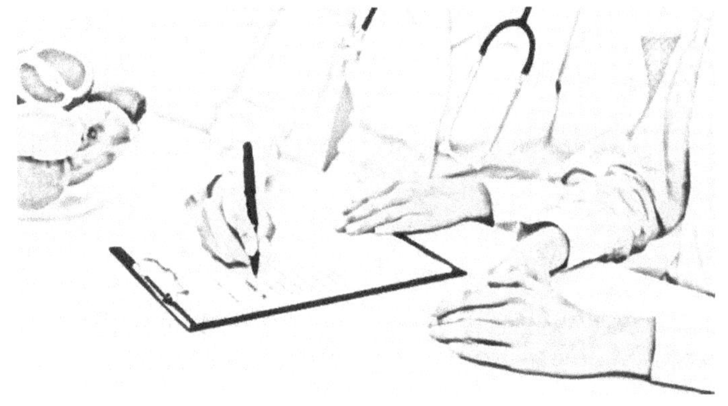

Here's a sample meal plan for a successful day on a NASH diet:

Breakfast

- Spinach and Mushroom Omelette
- 1 slice of whole-grain toast
- 1 cup of mixed berries

Morning Snack

- Greek Yogurt Parfait with granola and fresh berries

Lunch

- Grilled Chicken Salad with mixed greens, cherry tomatoes, cucumber slices, and balsamic vinaigrette
- 1 small sweet potato, roasted

Afternoon Snack

- Roasted Chickpeas

Dinner

- Baked Cod with Lemon and Herbs
- Quinoa and Roasted Vegetable Bowl
- Steamed broccoli

Evening Snack (optional)

- Banana Oat Pancakes with a drizzle of honey

Remember to stay hydrated throughout the day by

drinking plenty of water. Adjust the portion sizes according to your individual needs and consult with a healthcare professional or a registered dietitian for personalized meal planning and dietary recommendations.

This sample meal plan incorporates a variety of nutrient-dense foods while considering the dietary needs for NASH. It focuses on lean proteins, healthy fats, high-fiber carbohydrates, and plenty of fruits and vegetables. Enjoy these meals as part of a balanced and healthy eating routine to support your liver health.

Here's another sample NASH meal plan for a successful day:

Breakfast

- Overnight Chia Pudding with mixed berries and chopped almonds
- 1 boiled egg

Morning Snack

- Carrot Sticks with Hummus

Lunch

- Grilled Chicken Breast with a side of steamed broccoli and quinoa
- Mixed Green Salad with cherry tomatoes, cucumbers, and a drizzle of olive oil and lemon juice

Afternoon Snack

- Apple Slices with Almond Butter

Dinner

- Baked Salmon with a squeeze of lemon and dill
- Roasted Brussels Sprouts with garlic and olive oil
- Brown Rice

Evening Snack (optional)

- Chocolate Avocado Mousse

Remember to adjust the portion sizes based on your individual needs and consult with a healthcare professional or a registered dietitian for personalized meal planning and dietary recommendations. This sample meal plan provides a balance of lean proteins, healthy fats, whole grains, and plenty of fruits and vegetables to support your NASH dietary goals. Enjoy these meals as part of a nourishing and liver-friendly eating routine.

Here's another NASH meal plan for a successful day:

Breakfast

- Veggie Egg Muffins (made with spinach, bell peppers, and onions)
- 1 small whole-grain tortilla
- Sliced avocado

Morning Snack

- Celery Sticks with Almond Butter

Lunch

- Grilled Shrimp Skewers with a squeeze of lime
- Quinoa Salad with mixed vegetables (such as cucumbers, cherry tomatoes, and red onions) tossed in a light vinaigrette

Afternoon Snack

- Greek Yogurt with a sprinkle of granola and fresh berries

Dinner

- Baked Chicken Breast with herbs and spices
- Roasted Asparagus with garlic and olive oil
- Cauliflower Rice

Evening Snack (optional)

- Berry Smoothie made with unsweetened almond milk, mixed berries, and a handful of spinach

Remember to customize the portion sizes according to your individual needs and consult with a healthcare professional or a registered dietitian for personalized meal planning and dietary recommendations. This sample meal plan incorporates lean proteins, fiber-rich carbohydrates, and plenty of vegetables to support a NASH-friendly eating plan. Enjoy these meals as part of a nourishing and liver-supportive routine.

NASH DIET SUCCESS STORIES

Non-alcoholic steatohepatitis (NASH) is a liver condition that affects many individuals worldwide. The good news is that NASH can be reversible through the implementation of a NASH diet and positive lifestyle changes. In this chapter, we will share inspiring stories of individuals who have successfully reversed their NASH diagnosis through dietary modifications and lifestyle adjustments. These stories serve as a beacon of hope and motivation for those navigating their own journey with NASH.

Sarah's Remarkable Transformation

Sarah's struggle with NASH began when she was diagnosed with the condition at the age of 35. Faced with the potential consequences of her liver health, Sarah decided to take charge of her well-being. She committed herself to a NASH diet that focused on whole foods, reducing added sugars, and increasing her intake of fruits, vegetables, and lean proteins. Additionally, Sarah incorporated regular exercise into her routine, combining cardiovascular workouts with strength training. Over time, Sarah's dedication paid off as she witnessed a significant improvement in her liver function tests, decreased inflammation, and restored liver health. Today, Sarah continues to embrace a healthy lifestyle and serves as an inspiration to others on their NASH journey.

Mark's Journey to Health and Vitality

Mark's life took a positive turn when he received a diagnosis of NASH at the age of 45. Determined to reverse the condition, Mark embarked on a transformative journey. He began by making dietary changes, focusing on portion control, reducing saturated fats, and eliminating processed foods from his meals. Mark discovered the power of whole foods, incorporating colorful fruits and vegetables, whole grains, and healthy fats into his diet. Alongside his dietary modifications, Mark adopted an active lifestyle, engaging in regular exercise and increasing his physical activity levels. As a result, Mark experienced a significant reduction in liver inflammation, improved liver function, and a newfound vitality. Mark's journey serves as a testament to the positive impact that a NASH diet and lifestyle changes can have on overall liver health.

Emma's NASH Recovery Story

Emma's NASH diagnosis at the age of 50 was a wake-up call that propelled her into action. She embraced the NASH diet with determination, focusing on reducing refined carbohydrates, added sugars, and unhealthy fats. Emma incorporated nutrient-dense foods such as leafy greens, cruciferous vegetables, lean proteins, and anti-inflammatory spices into her meals. In addition to dietary modifications, Emma adopted stress-reducing techniques, such as meditation and yoga, to support her overall well-being. Over time, Emma experienced remarkable improvements in her liver function, decreased liver fat accumulation, and a renewed sense of vitality. Emma's story highlights the importance of a holistic approach to NASH recovery, encompassing both dietary changes and stress management strategies.

Michael's Path to Liver Health

Michael, a 48-year-old man, was diagnosed with NASH after experiencing persistent fatigue and abdominal discomfort. Determined to improve his liver health, Michael committed himself to a NASH diet and made significant lifestyle changes. He eliminated processed foods, sugary beverages, and unhealthy fats from his diet, focusing instead on whole, nutrient-dense foods. Michael started incorporating regular exercise into his routine, including strength training and cardio workouts. With time, dedication, and support from his healthcare team, Michael witnessed a remarkable improvement in his liver enzymes, reduced liver inflammation, and increased energy levels. Today, Michael continues to follow a NASH-friendly diet and lifestyle, maintaining his liver health and enjoying a renewed sense of well-being.

Olivia's Journey to a Healthier Liver

Olivia, a 35-year-old woman, was diagnosed with NASH during a routine check-up. Devastated by the news, she decided to take control of her health and embarked on a transformative journey. Olivia embraced a NASH diet that focused on whole foods, high-fiber carbohydrates, lean proteins, and healthy fats. She also incorporated regular physical activity into her daily routine, engaging in activities such as jogging, yoga, and swimming. Through her commitment to the NASH diet and a healthier lifestyle, Olivia experienced weight loss, improved liver function, and a reduction in liver fat accumulation. Her determination and perseverance serve as an inspiration to others facing the challenges of NASH.

Ethan's Lifestyle Overhaul for NASH Reversal

Ethan, a 55-year-old man, received a NASH diagnosis and was motivated to make significant changes to his lifestyle. He began by consulting with a registered dietitian to create a personalized NASH diet plan. Ethan focused on portion control, reducing his intake of refined sugars and carbohydrates, and incorporating more vegetables, lean proteins, and whole grains into his meals. In addition to dietary modifications, Ethan implemented regular exercise into his routine, including brisk walking and strength training. Over time, Ethan experienced weight loss, improved liver function, and a decrease in liver inflammation. His dedication to a NASH-friendly lifestyle showcases the transformative power of combining a healthy diet with regular physical activity.

These inspiring stories of individuals who successfully reversed their NASH diagnosis through diet and lifestyle changes illustrate the transformative power of taking control of one's health. By embracing a NASH diet, making conscious food choices, and incorporating regular physical activity, these individuals have achieved remarkable improvements in their liver health and overall well-being. Their stories serve as a testament to the fact that NASH is a reversible condition, and with dedication and perseverance, one can regain control over their liver health. Through the lessons and experiences shared in this chapter, we hope to inspire and motivate others on their own journey to overcoming NASH and achieving optimal liver health.

FREQUENTLY ASKED QUESTIONS

What is the NASH diet?

The NASH diet is a dietary approach specifically designed to support individuals with non-alcoholic steatohepatitis (NASH), a liver condition characterized by inflammation and fat accumulation in the liver. The diet focuses on consuming whole, nutrient-dense foods while reducing the intake of added sugars, refined carbohydrates, saturated fats, and processed foods. It emphasizes fruits, vegetables, whole grains, lean proteins, and healthy fats.

Can the NASH diet help with weight loss?

Yes, the NASH diet can be effective for weight loss. By emphasizing whole foods and reducing calorie-dense and processed foods, the NASH diet promotes a healthy balance of nutrients and helps create a calorie deficit, which is essential for weight loss. It is important to consult with a registered dietitian or healthcare professional to personalize the NASH diet and ensure a safe and sustainable weight loss plan.

Is exercise important for NASH management?

Regular exercise is an important component of NASH management. Physical activity helps promote weight loss, improve insulin sensitivity, reduce liver fat accumulation, and enhance overall liver health. Aim for a combination of cardiovascular exercises, such as walking, jogging, or cycling, along with strength training exercises to build muscle and support metabolic health.

Can stress affect NASH progression?

Stress can have an impact on NASH progression and overall liver health. Chronic stress can lead to increased inflammation, worsen insulin resistance, and negatively affect metabolic health. Therefore, stress management techniques, such as mindfulness meditation, deep breathing exercises, and engaging in relaxing activities, are important for individuals with NASH.

Can the NASH Diet be personalized for specific dietary restrictions or preferences?

The NASH diet can be personalized to accommodate various dietary restrictions or preferences. Whether you follow a vegetarian, vegan, gluten-free, or dairy-free diet, it is possible to modify the NASH diet accordingly. Consult with a registered dietitian or healthcare professional to develop a tailored meal plan that meets your specific needs while still adhering to the principles of the NASH diet.

How can I personalize the NASH Diet to fit my lifestyle?

The NASH diet can be adapted to fit your lifestyle by incorporating foods that you enjoy and finding creative ways to prepare meals. Experiment with different flavors, spices, and cooking methods to make your meals exciting and satisfying. It is also important to consider your daily schedule and plan meals in advance to ensure consistency and adherence to the NASH diet.

Are there any medication interactions I should be aware of when following the NASH Diet?

Some medications may interact with certain foods or supplements, so it is essential to consult with your healthcare provider or pharmacist regarding any potential interactions. They can provide guidance on adjusting your medication schedule or monitoring certain nutrients while on specific medications. Open communication with your healthcare team is crucial to ensure optimal management of your health conditions while following the NASH diet.

Can individuals with other medical conditions follow the NASH Diet?

The NASH diet focuses on healthy eating principles that can benefit individuals with various medical conditions. However, it is essential to consider any specific dietary restrictions or modifications required for your medical condition. For example, individuals with diabetes may need to monitor carbohydrate intake more closely. Consulting with a registered dietitian or healthcare professional will help you personalize the NASH diet to suit your specific medical needs.

Are there any supplements that can support liver health while following the NASH Diet?

Supplements should be approached with caution, as they are not a substitute for a healthy diet. However, certain supplements may support liver health when used in conjunction with a balanced diet. Common supplements include milk thistle, N-acetylcysteine, vitamin E, and omega-3 fatty acids. It is important to consult with a healthcare professional before incorporating any supplements into your regimen to ensure safety, appropriate dosage, and consideration of any potential interactions with medications.

Can the NASH diet be followed long-term?

The NASH diet is designed to be a long-term approach to support liver health and overall well-being. It emphasizes sustainable dietary changes and a healthy lifestyle. It is not a short-term fad diet but rather a way of eating that promotes optimal liver function and maintenance of a healthy weight. Consult with a registered dietitian or healthcare professional for ongoing guidance and support in following the NASH diet long-term.

Is it necessary to continue the NASH diet after NASH reversal?

Once NASH has been successfully reversed, it is important to maintain a healthy lifestyle, including a balanced diet and regular physical activity, to prevent the reoccurrence of NASH. Transitioning to a maintenance plan that incorporates the principles of the NASH diet can help sustain liver health and reduce the risk of NASH relapse.

TOWARDS A PROMISING FUTURE FOR PEOPLE WITH NASH

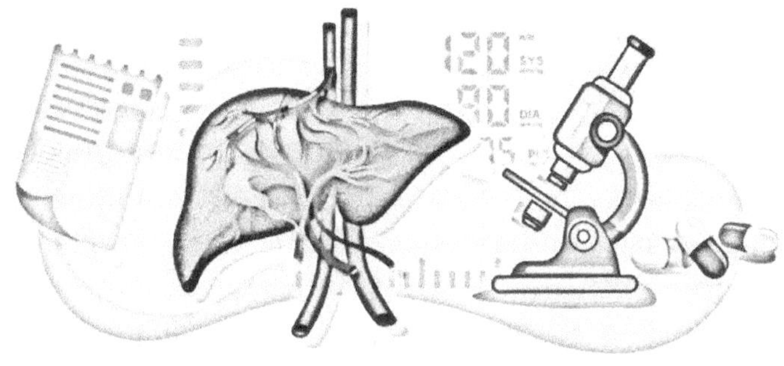

In this final chapter, we'll explore the prospects and promising advances in the understanding and treatment of NASH. As the prevalence of the disease continues to rise worldwide, researchers, clinicians and the pharmaceutical industry are actively working to find new treatment strategies and innovative solutions to help people with NASH manage their condition and improve their quality of life.

Advances in Research

Research into NASH has advanced considerably in recent years, leading to a better understanding of the disease's underlying mechanisms. Studies have identified several potential therapeutic pathways and targets, paving the way for the development of specific new drugs to treat NASH. In addition, research into biomarkers and advanced diagnostic tools is enabling earlier detection of the disease and more accurate monitoring of its progression.

Emerging therapeutic Approaches

New classes of drugs are currently being developed to treat NASH. These drugs target different aspects of the disease, such as inflammation, fat accumulation in the liver and liver fibrosis. Some drugs have already shown promising results in clinical trials, offering hope for future, more effective treatments. However, it is important to note that the safety and efficacy of these drugs must be thoroughly evaluated before they are widely available to patients.

The Importance of education and Support

As research and treatments progress, it's essential to stress the importance of education and support for people with NASH. Education programs can help patients better understand their condition, associated risk factors and self-management strategies, including lifestyle changes and regular follow-up with healthcare professionals. In addition, emotional and social support can play a crucial role in disease management, enabling patients to share their experiences, find support and reinforce their motivation to take care of their health.

The NASH landscape continues to evolve rapidly, offering hope and encouraging prospects for people with this disease. As research continues and new treatments emerge, it's important to stay informed, work closely with healthcare professionals and take active steps to support our liver health. Together, we can build a bright future for people with NASH, by improving treatment options, promoting prevention and supporting those living with the disease.

EPILOGUE

Congratulations! You have reached the end of this book on the NASH diet.

In this book, we explored in detail the NASH diet and its importance in the management of non-alcoholic fatty liver disease. We've examined the key principles of the NASH diet, including foods to favor and avoid, as well as beneficial dietary supplements. We also shared inspiring testimonials from people who have successfully improved their liver health by adopting a healthy lifestyle and following a tailored diet.

NASH is a complex condition that requires a holistic approach to health. Clearly, our diet plays a crucial role in the progression of the disease and our ability to manage it effectively. By choosing nutritious foods rich in antioxidants, omega-3 fatty acids and lean protein, we can support our liver health and reduce inflammation. By avoiding processed foods rich in saturated fats and added sugars, as well as alcohol consumption, we can reduce risk factors and preserve our well-being.

However, it's important to note that every person is unique, and it's crucial to consult a healthcare professional before starting any diet or dietary supplement. They will be able to assess your specific health status, give you personalized advice and help you set up a NASH management plan tailored to your individual needs.

In addition to diet, it's essential to stress the importance of regular exercise, stress management, maintaining a healthy body weight and managing risk factors associated with NASH, such as diabetes and obesity.

The NASH diet represents an effective approach to the management of non-alcoholic fatty liver disease. By adopting a healthy lifestyle, making judicious food choices and benefiting from appropriate medical follow-up, it is possible to take control of your health and improve your quality of life.

Remember, your journey towards optimal liver health is unique, and results may vary from person to person. Celebrate your achievements, no matter how small, and stay motivated even during challenging times. Be patient with yourself and allow for gradual progress. Remember that each step you take towards a healthier lifestyle is a step towards a brighter future.

Finally, share your story! Your experiences, challenges, and triumphs can inspire and support others who may be facing similar journeys. Your voice matters, and by sharing your NASH journey, you can create a ripple effect of hope and empowerment.

As you close this book, carry with you the knowledge, inspiration, and determination to make positive choices for your liver health and overall well-being. Embrace the power of the NASH diet and the potential it holds to transform your life. You have the ability to reclaim your health, rewrite your story, and create a vibrant future.

Wishing you a life filled with vibrant health, happiness, and a thriving liver!

DO IT NOW

SOMETIMES 'LATER' BECOMES 'NEVER'